XAMISSA:
THE WATER
ARCHIVES

HENK ROSSOUW

Published by Akashic Books
©2018 Henk Rossouw

ISBN: 978-1-61775-630-6

Printed in China through Four Colour Print Group, Louisville, Kentucky
First printing

Akashic Books
Brooklyn, New York, USA
Ballydehob, Co. Cork, Ireland
Twitter: @AkashicBooks
Facebook: AkashicBooks
E-mail: info@akashicbooks.com
Website: www.akashicbooks.com

African Poetry Book Fund
Prairie Schooner
University of Nebraska
110 Andrews Hall
Lincoln, Nebraska 68588

TABLE OF CONTENTS

PREFACE

by Gabeba Baderoon

If you listen closely, landscape will confess its histories. And so Genade, Genadendal—Mercy, Valley of Mercy—towns in South Africa's interior, tell of the relentless violence of their naming only obliquely, and despite themselves. In the 1990s, the poet Sandile Dikeni led Monday night poetry readings at a place in the center of Cape Town called Café Camissa. Both poetry and the capacity to recover history's untold cruelties found a home in *Xamissa*, the name "crossed out" beneath the one we know, *Cape Town*. In Henk Rossouw's stunning collection of this name, *Xamissa: The Water Archives*, crossed out histories refuse their erasure, spill their liquid meaning, and reclaim the name that means "place of sweet waters."

> *Eish!* Xamissa not a place but water itself,
> archival, open as the city in May
> when the streets are water again

Eddying, disorienting, unforgotten, ceaselessly coursing, the history that the city wants to lose returns liquidly, wearing away, accreting, unburying. Since what you see when you look at this place is too easy at first, you might miss that its bright surfaces are like "a beautiful wet bag over the mouth of."

Xamissa: The Water Archives misses nothing. Cape Town's subterranean depths flow beneath cemented-over canals, hollowing out terms like *reclaimed ground* and *city of corporations.*

Listening to, walking in, inhabiting the city called Cape Town, the speaker in *Xamissa* enters along streets looped with telephone lines that copy the "sine waves" flight paths of the hundreds of "shadow-bodied" starlings above the city. Both copies and the hundreds of originals cloud perception, draw the gaze to unnoticed parts, the eaves of roofs, the parking lot of the Slave Lodge, the city's museum of slavery. Landscape is confession. Anything but surface.

The streets emerge
beside the canals

        …

The canals are buried
water   time's ossuary,

in a city imposed upon
shell middens, littoral

Water is history.

In the haze of past and present, flickering sky and skyline, you see and don't quite see a bus drive past on the way to its destination, Lost City. Language, the poems say, both denies and admits this history, the two insistently connected.

Xamissa, the city at nightfall double-lit
                                by the artificial and the fleeting.

In these poems, the city is a copy of itself, a machine of distraction hiding itself in "crossed out language." "The Water Archives" are made from limning such absences, following the signs of the starlings hovering in clouds over certain buildings, listening to the uncensored thetha (talk) on the street where we hear the underside of the Cape Town brochures. Free-flowing bile against "that sell-out tief (bitch)," and threats to kak (shit) on her gentoo (whore's) palace on the way to sebenza (work).

In the US, the speaker suddenly knows that the paths he is walking are "simultaneous with these footsteps" a continent away in Cape Town. In "The Water Archives" the speaker returns to read his own implication in erasure, in what is spoken, listened to, written. In a place built of "utterance / and creole echoes," the speaker recognizes that "my brother and I [are] morphemes / in the sentences of the city."

Lines refuse ease, sentences refuse to end, blanks refuse to be filled in. Signs for *BLANKES / NIE-BLANKES, WHITES / NON-WHITES* marked all apartheid landscapes, since the Afrikaans word for *white* is *blank*. Perfectly hiding and perfectly revealing itself, the nothingness of *BLANK* calls attention to itself in uppercase letters.

> a suspended desire line
> above Rolihlahla Boulevard   —renamed for the president
>
>
> imprisoned
>   on the island often
> visible from here.

Desire lines, the name for unofficial paths made gradually visible through thousands of footfalls, allow Rossouw to track a testament to freedom in the Cape Archives from court testimony given in 1808 by the slave Louis van Mauritius; thirty years before slavery finally ends to Nelson Mandela's speech at the Rivonia trial in 1964, lines made by words accrete force through being said thousands of times by thousands of voices.

> Xamissa is   sprachbund, city of utterance
>
> and creole echoes, none more Xamissa than
>
> the dialectic of now-now and just now—
>
> *now-now,* a little sooner than soon, not right now, I'll be there now-now
>
> *just now,* an indefinite time in the future, you shall be freed just now.

Xamissa's archives are "crossed out" histories: a photograph of Roggebaai beach now concreted over, words of slaves captured in court records, and the fact that the language of the city has a term for the indefinite lag between *just* and *now*; between *freed* and *just* and *now*. That uncrossed space is "none more Xamissa than."

REARRIVAL

1.

The loops of telephone wire   on creosote poles

copy—in dusk-lit

      sine waves—the arcade
flight pattern of the city

starlings. Red-winged, shadow-bodied birds

cloud the stone courtyard of the Dutch East India Company's Slave Lodge

and parking garages and eaves. This is

civil twilight. I have been absent for seven years.

Murmuration—
      collective noun for the cloudburst of starlings in the early winter sky,

my brother says. Starlings on the telephone wires line the foothill streets of
Walmer Estate. Our roadside perception of the houses and warehouses and lots,
sloping toward the harbor below, has been anchored momentarily among

      the crowd on the footbridge,
once segregated (*BLANK-
ES / NIE-BLANKES*) with legislative
sheet metal, and now

      a suspended desire line

above Rolihlahla Boulevard   —renamed for the president

imprisoned
          on the island often
visible from here.

The tarmac with his name contours against the table-shaped mountain as it
bisects the city.

Xamissa vs. Cape Town, the city in the brochure, little more than
          a summer dress, all air, colour and light, cast off onto

the indigenous peninsula—like a beautiful wet bag over the mouth of.

Hoerikwaggo means, in the crossed out language, mountain in the sea.

The Standard Bank sign on the foreshore

—cement land reclaimed from the sea and the descendants of enslaved
Xamissans, who would launch slender fishing boats there, from the shoreline
now buried under rubble—

flickers on blue against the close of day.

Xamissa, the city at nightfall double-lit
                                        by the artificial and the fleeting.

Electric sunset. The early

sodium-vapor street lamps echo the burnt orange.

2.

Domestic servants leaving Walmer Estate
cross the footbridge

in their nightly katabasis downhill.
       Shoprite bags in hand or balanced

on their heads—wages tithed to get home
to Lavender Hill, Mitchell's Plain, Lost City, Khayelitsha, Langa, Gugulethu

outside the city gates—
as the touts in the white
minibus taxis

echo the muezzin:
   Vredehoek, Vredehoek, Vred'hoek, W-a-a-a-a-a-a-a-a-a-lmer.

3.

From the footbridge, my brother and I look at the city

in silence. Daylight has not yet left

                              the avocado-green facade
of Ghazala Food & Kaffie
on the corner—   the corner of—   and day glow
vies with the fluorescent-lit   shelves—

soap   matches   pilchards

stacked behind the shopkeeper at rest in the doorway, marking time until the
tidal   hiss of the 102 bus. Some cross the city for his cumin samosas.

On the roads below
        Melbourne and Roodebloem,
narrowing downhill,
the stoeps on either side

        darken first.

You must be hungry, my brother says. I have aged
without him.

He lives near the abutment
of the bridge—   starlings in his attic,

and the dock cranes, new since
democracy, frame the sea as if

to lower the sun, a starboard-red
container, beyond the coastal   shelf.

The shipping line of sunlight   leaving for

4.

In the city,   begin
and begin again

sleep's graffiti

5.

*The city is tidal. In the day, people
stream into the city to sebenza, to thetha,
to be here by the sea. I take the bus from
Philippi for over two hours to get to high
school here. At night, the tide of us
departs and it's the umlungu sea-foam
city again,   the white crest ncinci.*

(Songo Tinise

Umlungu, in Xhosa, both
sea-foam   and whiteness.

        I recur in the city, song-lit

in the tidal city,   sea-foam
outpost at low tide

now the Cape, now Xamissa—

perhaps urban legend, it means

place of sweet waters,   plural
for the sake of its springs—

                the water archives

incipient on the mountainside,

artesian and running

under the city   asleep.

6.

The city

separate as the sleep of another

7.

If one were scattered at the end,   from a cardboard urn
after the flood,   with a view of the sward descending
to the bights and the coves—   the sea-bitten coast

one was born far from,   one's beginning
forgotten—   a handful of South African ash—
even the ash would echo   names of water,

distant water: The Whaleback Ledge   Lighthouse
across the Piscataqua,   whose origins beyond
the harbor and the tidal mouth   split into Salmon Falls

and the Cocheco, *rapid foaming water*,   fed by the Ela,
the Mad, and the Isinglass—   rivers striated
by glacial ice   and rising from the Nubble and the cold rain,

ponds,   replacements?   For Xamissa, place of

DOPPLER SHIFT

1.

On the way to the kitchen, this sensation of walking again in Xamissa, the low-rise buildings, the inevitable pastel of salt-desaturated paint, are themselves in motion as if walking alongside up Long Street—of being in and among the city surrounded by its inhabitants heading to the Palm Mosque or Lola's or the Long Street Baths simultaneous with these footsteps, for a second, the present now seven hours ahead—

2.

In the archive a photograph of a lost earlier
image, 1890, the pedestrians now a blur,

       now wisps of movimento.

Time's walking river is long   (Kamau Brathwaite

Portuguese creole, the early franca of the Indian Ocean
trade in enslaved people   to fund the seafoam city of Cabo, Caab, Cape
Town.

Fezzes, snap-brims, head scarfs
        on the street that runs
        from the sea to the foot-

hills. Long Street! Where

the seafoam city, Xamissa se mense, free
for a night, would find the temporary
succor of cockfights, dice-games, prayer. In the 18th

c. the Palm Mosque had two palms
and at the doorsteps of the double-

stories—flat-roofed by ordinance

in fear of the Hanglip maroon polis,
who set the thatched
                iniquitous city   alight

—plank bridges lead across the sluit,
a shallow low-walled canal, and now

I walk on Long Street in double-time, at the speed of water, spring water, a

water archive entry,
its alacrity diverted
under the sidewalk,

the canal absent since the belle epoque gas leak   exploding, circa—

3.

Xamissa's chronotope—

      the middens of black
      mussels whose eaters

      cross-hatch ochre
         and begin, lithic,

a city in a sea-cave.

A *city of corporations*   (George Oppen
      and the grassland before

transhumant pasture

extrapolates itself
from potable water.

A city of storms—Adamastor

fails in *The Lusíadas*
to drown its advent.

The seafoam arrivals canalize
or cannabalize Xamissa, a city

of streambeds, cicadas, stony pines, quartzite.

The streets emerge
beside the canals

BuitengrachtBuitensingelBuitenkant

outside canal, outside crescent, outside
side, and the seafoam outsiders separate

land from water   rights.

The canals are buried
water   time's ossuary,

in a city imposed upon
shell middens, littoral,

a city   unsanctioned

now—Royal Dutch Shell.

4.

If Xhosa borrows its clicks
from Xamissa's earliest
language, and in Afrikaans

eina! is also the Khoekhoe-
gowab utterance   for pain, then

in exchange for trade wind,
Xamissans return
the city to its first name

at night, pellucid or perhaps
    urban legend—
Xamissa or ‖*àm̃-mi* |*ʾáà-sä̀*

—to a name transliterated on behalf
of a language, an *X*-ed out language,

    the language of dilapidated stone

crosses. Smallpox? Small game?

The sea dark.

5.

In the '90s, ek sê,   I knew

two street kids, Ashraf and Stix,

flâneurs of small change and half-eaten KFC

     who'd aanklop the café tables on Long Street—
     kanala kanala—where time's walking river

is. Descendants of forced movimento over the sea?

The kids peroxide their afros

orange—the shade of sodium-vapor lamps.

Street life's about walking   (Ashraf

Ja, they call us strollers   (Stix

Strollers obsessed with cars.   One time

I gave Stix and Ashraf a driving lesson
    in the cable car parking lot above
the city, hoping to keep them okay
    next time they hijinked another
late-model Mercedes.

Knock before you come in   (Ashraf

about to doss outside in the doorway of Salon Capri.

Kanala kanala, they would say, echo
of canal or a loan-word from Malay?

Please or do me a favor, my friend Zackie tells me
        it means: A plea for hospitality, a signal
that we eat at the same café table

in the shadow of Table Mountain.

Stix was run over.   No one knows where

Ashraf is.

THE WATER ARCHIVES

1.

Above the city, leopard clouds—

     rosettes of immanent rain on the bright.

The crowd on Adderley St de-thronged
and fishless since

     the absence of the sea
in downtown Xamissa.

Roggebaai Beach haptic,
          unsegregated, open until.

Sand becomes concrete. Water into avenue.

     Beach Street | Strand Straat
     now a mile from its referent.

Demolished, *now a landscape, now a room*   (Walter Benjamin
     under the verandah. The crowd walks through

     the broken room of Louis   van Mauritius—leader

      in the uprising of

—and Anna, beloved.

At his trial, in 1808, Louis

predicts Rolihlahla @ Rivonia: *I had heard that in other countries*

all persons were free, and there were so many black people here who could
also be free, and that we ought to fight for our freedom and then, basta!

                              (Court of Justice 516, W. Cape Archives
Xamissa, the code-switch
                    of time?

The sea's erasure: run-up
act of apartheid to expel
black leisure. Axe the un-
segregated beach with
banks, highway, a sealed

harbor—

        now the fishless crowd sways to the second line of the distant sea.

2.

In a blink—0.0001 of a day

—my brother and I alight

        from the Golden Arrow bus

into a monkey's wedding, a sun shower

        in the city of iKapa, semi-
clouded, the leopard another guest.

Among the tidal
        convo, the delta
of pedestrians,

my brother and I morphemes

in the sentences of the city. Uthini? Eish, I sold my skorokoro. And the mayor,
that sell-out tief, I'll kak on the doorstep of her gentoo palace, right by the nice
brass knocker. J'ai marché plus de mille kilomètres pour arriver ici. Heita da!
Sharp-sharp. Jislaaik, the larneys are mos taking over alles now. Aweh, hoesit?
Duidelik.

Xamissa is   sprachbund, city of utterance

and creole echoes, none more Xamissa than

        the dialectic of now-now and just now—

now-now, a little sooner than soon, not right now, I'll be there now-now

just now, an indefinite time in the future, you shall be freed just now.

The glint of abalone at the bottom of the reissued canal that leads to the
        Waterfront mall,

of the twelve rix-dollars
per month,

Anna, free, must pay
Louis's eienaar until

just now;   justice.

3.

On crutches, my brother. Slow, we

cross the eddy of Adderley St.   Flotsam advert-
isements *TEKKIE TOWN* | Sneakerville   *ATLAS
FINANCE*   and someone inside the *CASH 4 GOLD*
sandwich board   snap-snaps her finger
against the handbill to catch

our attention in the rain, letters blotted. On the
          jaundice-yellow map, its photocopy
damp in my bag, the early Cape crowded with

watercourses and canals.

The urban legend—that before the Dutch

ships, the Cape was called

          Xamissa, *place of sweet waters*—

no more than El Dorado, a mistaken map:

in Khoekhoegowab, Nama, remnants
          now spoken in the desert to the north

||àm̋-mi, water |ʼáà-sä, fresh, new.

Eish! Xamissa not a place but water itself,

archival, open as the city in May
when the streets are water again,

now and again?   Xamissa, partially free, sidewalk wrinkled

in the people streams, my brother and I,

attached molecules—he the other *H* in our double bond, covalent, the crowd
on the street our *O*.

Cities are the contradictions of capitalism, spelled out in crowds
(Adam Gopnik

My brother works for Louis.
In the echo of uprising on
Strand St. To reclaim his city

not from the sea but the **VOC**.*

---

* Corporate logo of the V.O.C. or Dutch East India Company, 1602–1799.

4.

Feral rain. The flood light seeps through the curtain

in my brother's spare
bedroom. Sans

sleep—

     the farm where Louis van begins
     the uprising called Vogelgezang,

     Birdsong. One of the last streets
     left with its name in District Six.

     During the trial, Anna dies of—

I decide to gaze again, on my cellphone,   at *Roggebaai.jpeg*.

The bright, fish-laden boats. In the image, the scintillant

Roggebaai water.   Strand Street un-stranded. Domestic, interior—

Table Mountain
for eating under,

and as angular   as Garlics
Wholesale Warehouse.   Nets of dresses and rolled-up hems. The crowd

reflected in the damp sand   —Louis and Anna among

the distant waves just now?—a liminal city   afoot on the seabed for

a tidal instant,   without

the foam of whiteness.

Like Chaplin in *Modern Times* ended the era of silent comedy with the cicatrix
        of song, so too am I trampled

now-now

by your exodus, *O*
crowd of Xamissa.

I part the curtain, white muslin,   and witness, as if

The Flying Dutchman,

                a late bus—destination Lost City.